LIFE'S SEASONS OF JOY

By William Benedict

LOVE

LIFE

and

LIVE

Making a Difference

BY WILLIAM BENEDICT

ISBN 0-7414-0785-X

Published by:

INFINITY
PUBLISHING.COM

Infinity Publishing.com
519 West Lancaster Avenue
Haverford, PA 19041-1413
Info@buybooksontheweb.com
www.buybooksontheweb.com
Toll-free (877) BUY BOOK
Local Phone (610) 520-2500
Fax (610) 519-0261

Printed in the United States of America

Printed on Recycled Paper

Published September, 2001

Dedicated to those . . .

Looking for more meaning
And a more meaningful life.

And to Julia Benedict and
Louis Benedict—my parents,
Who never lived to know that
I had this interest in poetry.

Foreword

Life's Seasons of Joy is intended to bring expression and meaning, with the art of creativity. To reach all levels and all ages, *Life's Seasons of Joy* is to lift our minds and lift our sights. To bring more meaning to our lives and understanding. To let the simple and everyday things speak to us. To let the windows of our eyes be opened. To be captivated momentarily, but to be set free with enlightenment. With the aim of filling our searchings and longings. To give us more reasons to hold onto the realities.

There are conditions, circumstances and surroundings in our day and in our time. But we are not to let these control our lives. For each person is special. It is up to each of us to bring that specialness about. The choice is ours to make. May *Life's Seasons of Joy* help you to see the difference. Let the window of your life be opened to more meaning and expression.

IN POETRY

THE WORDS ARE ALIVE

AND LIVE

CONTENTS

BEGINNINGS, GLIMPSES, PORTRAYALS OF LIFE

THE ENCHANTMENT OF SPRING AND BEYOND

BEGINNINGS

GLIMPSES

PORTRAYALS

OF

LIFE

Life

The human being
Is like a vessel,
To fill in,
And pour out,

Never emptying,
And never
Quite filling,

But hoping,
With the best
Part of life,

And to serve a purpose,
On this journey,
That is life.

Learning About Life

As each day comes,
May it be with sunshine,
And make you
want to live.

For showers,
Make the flowers grow,
And you can bloom
from within.

The happiness in smiles,
Will reach across your face,
As the silent steps
that nature takes,
Are seen in every place.

And as the marks I trace with hope,
Arise within each day,
As I pause to see the peace,
Gently inviting me there.

My eyes trying to understand,
And I there learning,
Learning how to live,
Learning at each step.

In This Life

To live is to smile,
    And touch the sky,
And in the lowly earth
        to reach out,
To draw near as life passes,
To see on wings every season,
    Precious are beginnings
    As hope never ending,
To walk through every door,
    As some that may need opening,
To be there,
    Should there be a calling,
    And that voice to obey,
To find that happiness
    Which is all about,
To listen
    For every expression of joy,
To be there,
    Should there be a need,
For life
    Is a mark of action,
And the giving
    May be a part of ourselves,
        In this life,
            That we are to live,
        In this life,
            That we are to share.

If Only

If only I could
Keep the moments,
That surround each joy,

If I could only
Keep each day,
The meaning of life,
That holds me close,

To frame those pictures
Of endless love,
And thoughts that live,
As hope draws near,

If only today
Were tomorrow,
And time would not erase,

If only tomorrow
Were forever,
And time only a place.

In a Smile

In time
  We trust
 To live or die,
As days
  That spread
 Across our lives,

And to venture
  One day
 At a time,
So we might know
 And understand,

To grow and learn
  More each day,
To find the good
 Along the way.

Some words that touch
  Both day and night,
And to find the happiness
 To shine brightly,
  In a smile.

Principles of Life

The guiding principles of life,
Should they be of these,

Of letting the other person
Have first choice,
Of sharing,
In case there is a need,
Of telling in kind words,
Rather
Than bring distress,
The choice that has to be made,

Let principle stand,
And human error
Be put aside,
To go forward in peace,
To be
to each other
the joy of life,
And to be all,
you can be.

Footsteps

We journey
In the footsteps,
New and worn.

We journey in today
And wait for tomorrow
As are the visits
That pleases more,
The shortness of days
And reaching beyond,
The toil of night
That passes not.

Hope the possession
That enlightens the way,
To speak softly
As the morning dew,
To awaken
In each moment,
Today,
As our footsteps trace,
The faces and places,
That we have met.

What Is Read

Out there,
Is a place called time,
I find myself
haunted by,

In the morning
and the evening,
There are no fences
To mark the place,

Shadows
Mirrors
In each day,
A passing cloud
To mark each space,

Perhaps a season
to what is said,
And life
to what is read.

This Fear

The key to your mind
will unfold,

The road to your heart,

To turn your thoughts
rays of light,
To brighten your footsteps

In the night,

Shadows illuminating
the days of doubt,

To take away fear,
This feeling,
When I am afraid.

Eyes Shall See

The eyes shall see
    The morning light,
And seek the birds
    That rise in flight,

The whispers
        In cadence fly,
    Telling
        In the golden light,

The eyes shall not rest,
        In words
        In full array,
    To gently steal away,

Calling to paths
    That inspire,
        In the footsteps of tomorrow
        Beams in every morning.

Memories

As I drift
In memories lane,
I drift
In silent streams,

While birds that fly,
And raindrops fall,
I'll drift to far gone days,

For eyes did see,
For ears did hear,
Memories
how they pleased,

Some hard roads,
Some bending curves,
What joy at many turns,

Through Nature's Den
Heaven sent,
Still I often yearn,
The sounds of joy,
In endless ways,
To hold me,
Once again.

Learning to Learn

Let us not be fashioned
        or framed in ignorance,
Or the waywardness
        that may follow,
    To expel us
        from our dreams.

Let us not bring the impossible
    To the land of idleness,
        Lest we forget the emptiness
        When life serves no purpose.

Let us not forget the road
    Where we haven't been,
            The pain
                The toil
            The mind
        Life must forge.

And into that darkness
        Knowledge to bear,
And into that light
        Our banner to raise.

Meaning to Life

At the dawn of a new day
I awake with my eyes
Opening to a new start
in life

With the bow of faith
Stretching with hope
Aiming at those things
Hoping not to miss
in this life

For all those little things
They were so small
Sometimes I didn't see
I took for granted
But if they were not done
They would have been so big

The wind and rain that scatters
the plants to grow
My hands can hold
And I can taste
So many colors and shapes
To fill my wants and needs

Sometimes I have not the strength
To cover my faults
And I did make mistakes
I felt so little
That's when I wanted you to be so big
Big enough to forgive

When pain and sickness came
There was always someone
that cared
Even though it may have looked cloudy
And it didn't seem fair
I hoped all would be well in time

For all the laughter and joy
I have welcomed even with a smile
The hard road was made easy
Brought happy days
Brought strength
For all these and all of you
Have brought more meaning to life.

How to Live

The gift of life
Is like the gift of love,

The creativity of each one,
And not how much the gain,
For it asks nothing in return.

For life is to give,
What we may have,
And what,
We may learn,
In the day,
In the night,
Sometimes sacrifices
Have to be made.

As the barrenness speaks
of silence,
And reflects
the vividness,
Beyond is time.

To long
To yearn
To gather.
Hope renewing life,
And love in return,
And to show what life
Has meant to me.

Life Is to Live

Don't let life
pass you by,
In the quietness,
In the excitement.

Let the door of hope,
Open before you,
Which will always invite,
In the darkest of night.

To turn,
To all the living,
To let them tell,
what is life,
In all the beauty
That marks each day,
Traces to recall
in memories.

To gather for all seasons,
A time,
maybe when I am alone,
To know I have been,
A part of the living,
A part that is divine.

No Stranger

I am no stranger
To fear and doubt,
Uprisings within
And lonely nights.

I am no stranger
To being sad,
When darkness comes
And the roads are blind.

I am no stranger
To mountains high,
Where valleys greet
Laughing streams.

I am no stranger
To lost moments,
Time the echo
Of wasted days.

I am no stranger
To unkind looks,
Unsightly ways
That make things wrong.

I am no stranger
Only to self,
Selfish traits that harbor no gain
Perhaps only in strange ways.

In Passing of Time

Time,
Why do you leave me?
Joys should be long,
To welcome each day
Into the night,
To always please.

The peace,
In quiet moments
Reaching,
Quelling the fears,
Never thinking you
Will leave me.

To make happy
Each passing moment,
Coming to me in time,
Gathering often
To claim.

Time wait for me,
Help me to enjoy
To watch your ways,
To bring myself
In this life
To share,
To bring moments
To remember
Where I have been,
To the places
That will mean
Much to me.

We Are There

To tread deep waters
    Is it soul?
    Is it fear?
And hope
        that cares,
    Is it doubt?
The unwise
        that fails,
      The heights,
      The depths,
      Is it life?
    To cause
      To turn,
      To follow
        the sun,
The midnight hour,
Like some magic wand,
    Is it just,
      A passing cloud,
    Is it all,
    In all,

To gather them,
Or do we just follow,
      Only because,
      We are there.

Time

Time is the oasis of our life
The enchantment of each day
The measure of our stay
The echo till death.

Time
The pleasure,
The waste,
The embodiment
that clings.

The voice,
The mender,
The reminders
from day to day,
Time the beginning till the end.

Time we all have,
We share,
Time to time,
In our own way,
Time only time,
Will tell
What we have done,
Or what we have said.

Today

Often,
May it be today,
To smile,
To broaden the circle
of happiness,
To say a word,
To lift above the weights,
A word,
That may change directions,
and not in defeat,
Maybe to come as strangers,
Who is only a stranger
but for a moment,
To make someone happy,
Because you came by
this way today.

A Place in Time

Some stand tall
    and some alone,
Shadows linger
    where none follow,
He who marvels
    wanting hope,
Many stand
    where many roam,
Doubts have risen
    others fall,
The flight of echoes
    how few, how strong,
        This stature,
        This resolve,
    The command
In this fortress
        of time,
    Only the gallant,
    Only the strong,
Claiming this opulent
        place,
With high regard and
        triumphant,
    He stands tall,
    Who stands alone,
In the hands
    of unknown realms.

The Dead Ends of Life

The dead ends of life
Is it pain
Is it hurt
The aching heart
The lonely days,
Those things
That bring no joy,
Only sad faces,
The fear
The doubt,
Those empty lanes,
But will they last
In the rain.
The hopelessness
Of anger
Of senseless battles,
Of lost words
Of lost life,
To never be replaced,
The darkness
The shadows of no hope,
The emptiness and uselessness of life,
And struggles with no pay
or rewards,
As selfishness and pride,
A pattern that destroys,
From the hardness of our ways,
From the blindness of our eyes.

We Gaze

We gaze at the sunset
As clouds go rolling by,
The apple seed blend
In forest green,
Under the watchful eye,
A journey shadows
often reveal,
Ever so gently
My heart to please,
And the wayward things
That may beset my feet,
Sometimes,
Make me afraid.

Time Spent

Come
Say hello,
To someone
You do not know,

Come
Say hello,
To a flower
In full bloom,

Try to step aside,
To know
What is going on,

Around the corner
A different place,

Where time
Was spent,
Without you.

I Am

I am the echo of the past
I am the voice of the future
I am the garment
    That covers the present

I am life

I am the light
I am the darkness
I am the markings
    That cover the earth

I am life

I am the comings
I am the goings
I am the motions
    Of each day

I am life

This Plateau

Is there a plateau
    of every thought,
And action
    where to place,
Hope to take us there,
And doubt
    to flee away,
What is it
    that seems to be,
Which way
    shall I go,
The action
    and the setting,
To greet
    along the way,
For a time
    a gentleness pleasing,
And always joy
    to bring,
For hope
    has brought us here,
For such a time
    and for such a place,
Where time
    will have more meaning.

A Tribute

In the profoundness
of time and life,
Is it a journey
as if it were,
Reflecting
from time to time,
The images
in every measure,
Where and how far
is now or tomorrow,
Remembered perhaps when gone,
Not knowing
life is now,
Time not marking well,
The passages,
The monuments,
of each man.

How Do I Climb

I cannot climb the shadow
Nor the sunbeam,
Or the bow of the rainbow,

I cannot race the stars
Nor the light of day,
Or the darkness of the night,

I cannot know the height
Nor the depth,
    What matters is its breadth,

        I cannot
            I will not
            I do not know,
            What matters
            What really matters most.

In Life

Do I turn a corner
In high gear,
Or do I turn
At all?
When the grass
Is tall,
Or when
I cannot see?

Tell me when
The night falls,
How heavy
Will it be?
Might I not
Bear it,
Tell me
How to know.

The sunrise
The sunset,
Without any hands
To lay at rest,
Yet no one
Can put it there,
To tell
What part of day.

In the morning
In the evening,
To rise,
To go to bed,
No one
Now tells,
Only what is best.

For these
Are only words
You see,
Not the lines
In between,
For who knows
What you know,
Love
The highest trend.

Parting Ways

How the days have gone by
And the years slipped away,
Now it all seems only like yesterday,
Hoping now it will be different,
When I can wait for each morning,
To watch the world,
From my window,
To think of my friends
And maybe call them,
Talk about how it's been,
To now step aside
To live the life now that calls,
To measure time in another way,
Hoping to slow down, to fully enjoy,
Remembering
I have yet to live,
To be able to recall,
The footsteps in time,
And not have to count the years.

Anger

When anger comes,
Is it out of love,
The faults we find,
or wrongs?

The weary hard long day,
We bear so long,
Then breaks the tone.

The spell we dwell in
is shattered,
The calm slighted.

Through neglect
we sought the best,
Ourselves having faulted,
For reasons
We should have forgotten.

The void we filled,
With anger instead,
While patience got lost.

I Wonder

I do not count wealth
As a means of exchange,
Unless it can be shared
without the pain,
In hope that gathers
when I look up,
Time that is abundant
how life is paid,
Do we measure each day
By the things that we do,
Can we share a smile
To drop along the way,
The quietness that greets
At the end of the day,
When I stop to listen,
In a kind way,
Bringing thoughts
That do not go away,
Then it makes me wonder
when unaware,
Will happiness return?
To find
a place to stay.

Peace

What is peace?
The peace
That takes our mind away,
From stress
Doubt
And fear,
Away to not listen
To these wedges,
That want to
Break us apart,
So we walk away
Leaving the ugly scene,
To look for a place
That is serene,
We look for Spring
To fill our eyes,
To fill some dreams,
Coming in a summer's
dream,
We look for people
To take us away,
To fill our minds
With pleasant
things,
To bring us peace,
In silent ways.

The Flight

I want to reach
up to the sky,
And touch the heights
a bright star,
Radiant light
to gather around,
To just dream
On lonely nights.

I want to reach
the quietness,
If I had wings
to go again,
To places where doubt
has found the peace,
There to never leave.

I want to walk
the traversed road,
Where time will take
beyond all hope,
To never know
the darkened night,
Shadows reaching
always for light.

Moving beyond
the distance of time,
Sun, moon and stars
faintly the cosmos,
The years go by so quietly
the seasons often tell,
The plight that nature seeks
and man often tries to keep,
Watching time fly.

The Reason

While the day was full of love and care,
I was left with doubt and fear,
Shadows racing unaware,
Thoughts that seemed beyond control,
Echoes passing through the sky,
Each word measured long and wide,
The depths that deepen day and night,
As if there are no lines to grasp,
The stillness bears its weight on time
But what is there to cling on hope,
The touch that lifts and holds the weak
The lonely moments scatter dreams,
Where the light shines full and bright
The darkness seeks and gathers round,
But Oh the joy,
when there is peace,
The night is gone and life is sweet,

Climbing to mountain peaks,
Searching with a kind of yearning,
Knowing all must end,
And a mark is left,
To show the reason.

The Trend

Life is a window
One passes through,
In the day
In the darkness,
May love be shining through.

Where time measures,
Where hope often comes,
A story that has no limit
Until death is due.

When I reach
When I go,
A fathom never to return.

Hope that reaches
To unknown ways,
High above
Common reason.

When troubles come
When joys come in,
How can one
Keep that happy trend.

Man's Freedom

Never before
    On the face of the earth,
Has a torn people
    From oppression
    And with renewed hope,
Having gathered
    From many lands
Sought a new beginning,
    New in thoughts
    New in aspirations,
Having melted
    Their diversities
        of background,
But with the same intent
    Of mind, to be free,
Which is peace in the soul,
To let that inner man
    Become a reality,
        In face of perplexities,
    No matter how complex,
Reaching out of darkness
  Encompassing free thought,
Freedom,
    Which has been man's
        Supreme being.

The Enchantment of Spring and Beyond

At Dawn

At dawn
I saw the sun rise,
Cast its rays of hope.

The spell of darkness fleeing,
To where
No one knows.

I saw the beams of sunshine,
Take up Nature's song,
The brightness to gather round,
Around in heaven's glow.

A Whisper

Whisper to me
Gentle Spring,
In tenderness
and tenderly.

With rays
of gold,
To light my way,
To brighten
This lonely face.

Bring the freshness
of my wears,
As fresh as Spring
and some
Kind thoughts.

To lift the darkness
From my soul,
To know
That life is real.

Touch of Sun

The touch of the sun
With its warmth and glow,
Gathers all the flowers to grow,

The touch of the sun
Lights the darkened way,
That takes away the night of day,

The touch of the sun
Smiles in a funny way,
Brings laughter and joy
Like a day in May,

The touch of the sun
Finds a place to stay,
Brings in love,
That does not fly away.

The Flowers

I long for the flowers
that bloom in May,
The warmth of love
that follows each day,
To come with gladness
the sweet refrain,
And to know
Each moment
of every day.

And to dwell,
Where unmeasured bounties
are without fail,
Unless should I fail
to see them,
About,
And along the way.

Walk in the Presence

Walk in the presence of the living
    Bathe in its freshness at Spring,

Follow the shadows of dawn
    Always reaching out to touch,

The music that sways in chorus
    Heard in the echoes of morning,

        Passing from death to life,
            Rejoicing
                In song as Spring,

      And I to follow the yearnings,
        Trying
            Step by step.

The Wonders

Who discovered the sun
That was always there?
And the darkened path
That follows the night?
The brightest beam
To that shinning star?
Where all the glows
Are repeated in sounds?
The shores that are mapped
Around the earth?
To gather for storms
Upon human hearts?
The radiance in each flower
Eyes to behold?
Wonders that gather about each day,
And lifting our spirits
Beyond in hope,
Needing only
To know the way.

In the Fullness

Like a mighty wind,
That swept over my soul,
As gentle raindrops
Gathered above,

Speaking of things
Around me,
To feather my happiness,
As I looked
To behold.

The goodness
In the earth . . .

The joys
From within . . .

In the fullness
of my soul,
And in the fullness
of the earth.

Silence

Silence
has no regrets,
or sad responses,

Only high mountains
and refrains,

Sonnets
of flowing streams.

Nature Says It Best

If nature says it best,
Man tries to understand
By trying to relate,

The heights,
The depths,
The closeness
To the heart
Each breath,
The nearest to explain,
The fullness
Is man's endeavor
To acclaim.

Words
and
Feelings
A glowing part of life,
Hidden so often
Along the way,
As if life
Is the expression,
Of a special moment.

Raindrops

I hear raindrops
Or are they tears,
Bringing Nature's
Loving care,
Bringing joys
To have been there,
To listen,
To recall,
Moments
when sadness
Is wiped away in tears,
Or joys marked
To remember
To wipe away our fears.

Come with Me

Come---
To the river
To the spring
To the mountain
To see the majesty

Come with me
To the stillness
To hear the whispers
The silence
The rhapsody of night

Listen
Listen to the gentleness
That indescribable voice
that speaks
While walking through
the sounds
Of light and darkness
While walking to the moon

Come with me
To a time you cannot
measure
You may not hold
Perhaps for only but
a moment
Like the desert rain
Where has it gone
Gone with time
Only to come again
To refresh the earth in Spring

The Voice I Hear

I heard a song
That reminds of Spring,
Willows and daffodils,

I heard the clouds
Ensuing shadows,
Lightening and falling rain,

I heard the darkness rolled away,
Pressed to the earth below,
And shadows that seem to say,
Find me if you can,

I heard a whisper
Peace and joy,
The ark of knowledge
That opens doors,

I heard the voice
Of flowers sing,
To fill my inward sky
With dreams,

To wait upon the flight of time,
To carry through
This life of mine,

I long for all
There is of life,
Hoping to choose well
In each day.

Will Spring Come

Will
Spring
Come
On a midnight's bed,
On a lonely vigil,
On a path not worn,

Will
Spring
Come
On a quiet steed,
In an open window,
Lifting from the earth below,

In heaven's blend,
To draw within,
The joys of hope
To endless praise,

Will
Spring
Come
Come some day,
To remind me,
Of all the things,
That make
For a better place
And make
For a better time.

Oh Spring!

Oh Spring
so near,
Where are
Your whisperings?
The call
You bring,
The dawn
Birds sing,
And happy moments
Flowers brim,

Oh where,
Is your cloth
So neat,
Bringing joys
That cling?

Spring Will Come

Though the course of time
Drifts us apart,
Though your voice
Seems so far away,

I know one day
It will be Spring,
And your song
Will be heard again.

For now,
I shall wait,
I know your innocence
will be true,
Reminding me
of other years.

And when near,
I will listen more closely,
With each passing year,
Although,
Should I part,
Never to hear your voice,
I know you will come again,
And I do not
Have to wait.

Yet the Stillness

The stillness
Brought flowers,
Brought death,
Outside of every window,
Life passing by
To some the end.

Shadows in silence speak,
Haunting to some
The mind,
Left in a void,
Unexplained.

Yet, the stillness gropes,
Marking along the way,
Stretching beyond
Mountains and peaks,
Touching each day,
Like the sun,
That is never heard.

At Night

When I lie
Awake at night,
The stars do sing
Their songs of praise.

And if I fail
Not to hear,
The darkness lifts
Their silent notes.

And high above
If I could reach,
The midnight shores
Of pleasant dreams.

If only to hear,
Their silent steps,
Echoes that seem,
To always charm.

I Saw

I saw no path
    Across the sea,
No road to follow
        Or to chart,

I saw the same
    In the sky,
Not a trace,
    And not even a mark,

To see,
To listen,
    The vanishing
        of things,

And in the sky
    no measure,
        To outreach.

The Darkness

The night is a song
To never forget,
Through the eyes of many,
To some, that never know.

The stillness following
The silent refrain,
Hastening not in vain.

Steps may falter,
Whispers heard,
This giant saying,
Come to me.

Shadows nigh
By unheard ears,
The breeze echoing,
Do come to me.

This song
Can you hear.
The melody touching,
A shout!
Don't shut the door.

This body of darkness,
This fathom delight,
Enraptures my soul,
In the passing of night.

This symphony
This sovereignty
Empowering
The whole earth.

Gentle Wind

Wandering wind
On a summer's day,

Whispers,
In the cool
of night,

Softly treading
In unseen faces,
In passages,
Unknown.

My Eyes

The landscape
That fills
My eyes,

No hands can make,
The rocks
and running streams,

While clouds and skies
Seem to flee away,
Or is it
in my mind,
Wanting them to stay.

The Wind

Down canyons
And valleys,
And unsuspecting minds,
To venture
To heights,
Gathering the clouds

Gentle as the breeze,
Gentle as the heart sees,

Sees the running wind,

The unsuspecting eye
That sees
And feels,
Not knowing the way
of the wind,

Not knowing
the path it takes.

Distance and Time

Is going away
In distance and time

As flowers and streams
Keep reminding me

As these thoughts
Keep taking me back

Remembering mostly joys

Where I started
Having gained much

And the surroundings
I like to call friends
As these will always remain

And remind me
Where I have been

Leaving traces
And patterns
Hoping to return

Like flowers
    And streams
        In Spring

Walking in my mind
  When I think of them

When Summer Comes

I'll cast my stance
In shadows' lace,
And drift
In silent lanes,
And high above
Where
Sunbeams trace,
Embrace
The sands of time
Each day,
I'll climb
The notes
That reach beyond,
The dawn
and return,
To gather once
Both short
and tall,
The lengths
of life
each day.

Summer's End

Summer ---
You have said your piece,
So the geese
are flying south,
The birds are rounding up
To more than just a crowd,
The leaves are now fading
In the sunset of colors,
The majesty of Autumn
In the mountains and the valleys,
But soon the voice of Winter
Will soon be on its way,
While the landscape falls asleep,
Who will mourn
on bending knee,
Who will mourn for this body
that is now laid to rest,
Who will now gather
For the birds
have gone away,
For the barrenness of nature
Now sheds
None of Summer's joy,
For you see this house is empty,
The geese
have flown away.

Longing for Spring

I longed for Spring
When Autumn came,
For I longed for life,
The now fading face,
I was taken away,
From the reality of Spring
I went.

I longed for the fragrance,
The newness,
The beginnings,
I longed for Spring
I longed from death,
I longed for the longings
Instead was the grave,

Blind
When I came,
The newness now was gone,
The approaching has passed,
My footsteps faltered,
And I was lost,
For I longed for Spring
I longed for life,
From the reality of Spring
I went.

Autumn's Love on Wings

Like the leaves of autumn
Falling silently,
Perhaps even unnoticed,
The beauty of colors warmly rest
The touch graced in sunlight best.

Gone is the wind
Secretly hiding,
Lost in the maze
Of quiet evenings,
Where footsteps trace
There are not steps,
Only the warmth
Clothed in days.

Gone is tomorrow
In yesterdays,
Gone like a shadow
Is love's embrace,
As echoes of the past
Sound in memories,
Feelings sometimes
Shed in tears.

Gone
Gone
The rainbow in beauty,
In forever
Is love's image,
Love a voice
That is always near,
A shadow
That does not turn away.

Falling Shades

I'm talking
about leaves,
Small bouquets
Candles hold,
The ones falling
from a tree,
I'm talking about
the ones I rake,
The ones knee deep,
The ones
No artist
can paint,
I'm talking about
Autumn's face,
That is hard
To erase,
And the joy
That it brings.

Nature

Nature sings
Nature brings
Nature's green
	In many things

Nature is colors
Nature is yellow
Nature says it best
	In red

Nature loves Spring
Nature longs for Summer
Nature wonders
	In the Winter

Nature is life
Nature is alive
Nature has
	No off season